JENNY LIND
Songbird from Sweden

JENNY LIND

SONGBIRD FROM SWEDEN

by Elisabeth P. Myers

illustrated by Frank Vaughn

GARRARD PUBLISHING COMPANY
Champaign, Illinois

J
927.8
L

Photo Credits:

James Barrie from *A Biography of Jenny Lind*
   by Joan Bulman, copyright 1956:   pp. 63, 128
Danish Information Service: pp. 1, 67
Historical Pictures Service, Chicago: pp. 41, 54, 69, 75, 80,
   82, 89, 92, 101, 111, 113, 134
The New York Historical Society, New York City: pp. 105, 109, 118, 125, 138
New York Public Library: p. 103
Swedish Information Service: p. 2

Contents

1 Fanfare for Jenny

The sharp clear call of a blackbird came from a tree in the Ferndals' garden in Sweden. Three-year-old Jenny Lind, sitting on the grass making a daisy chain, echoed the call. It was spring, 1823.

Jenny's foster father, Carl Ferndal, was standing beside an open window in the house nearby. He heard both calls and smiled.

"Bless the child!" he said. He turned to look at his wife, who was lying on a couch near him. "Singing comes as naturally to Jenny as breathing, doesn't it, my dear?"

Karen Ferndal nodded and sighed. "She is

like a ray of sunshine around the place. How we shall miss her."

"That we shall," said Carl. "I couldn't love her more if she were our own daughter. But the doctor says you are not strong enough now to care for an active child. The boys and I can't give a little girl the motherly attention she needs."

Tears began to roll down Karen's cheeks. "Oh, Carl, do you think Anna Maria will mother her?"

Carl looked down at the floor. "Anna Maria is Jenny's real mother—"

"But Jenny was only two weeks old when Anna Maria brought her to us. How often since then has she come to visit her baby?"

"Not often," Carl admitted.

"And when she did come, she wanted Jenny to call her 'Aunt,'" Karen reminded him.

"Well, perhaps she didn't want to confuse Jenny," Carl suggested. "After all, Jenny has been taught to call you 'Mama'—and to call me 'Papa' ever since she could talk."

He stretched out a comforting hand. Karen took hold of it tightly.

"We must be glad we've had Jenny this long," Carl said. "We've given her three years of love and of carefree country life."

"But I'm so afraid she'll be unhappy in Stockholm, Carl. Just imagine Jenny cooped up in a city house! It's like putting a wild bird in a cage!"

As if the word "bird" had been a signal, the call of the blackbird sounded again. Again Jenny echoed it. Then came another sound — that of carriage wheels rumbling over a wooden bridge.

"That must be Anna Maria!" Karen cried. "I must go to Jenny." She tried to sit up, but she was too weak. She fell back against her pillows.

"I'll bring Jenny to you," Carl said.

He left the room quickly. When he returned Anna Maria as well as Jenny was with him.

"I can't stay, Karen," Anna Maria said bluntly. "As soon as Carl gets Jenny's things, we'll be on our way."

Karen held out her arms. "Jenny, come kiss me," she said.

Jenny went to her willingly. Karen stroked the little girl's corn-colored hair and looked lovingly into her gray-blue eyes. "Don't forget to say your prayers."

Jenny didn't understand. "If I did, you'd remind me," she said. "Wouldn't you, Mama?"

Karen shook her head. "I won't be there to remind you, Jenny."

"There?" echoed Jenny. "Where, Mama?"

Carl Ferndal answered for his wife. "In Stockholm, Jenny. You—you're going there with Anna Maria."

"There's been enough talk," Anna Maria said. "Carl, get Jenny's things. I want to be home in time for supper."

Carl held out his hand to Jenny. "Come help me, Jenny," he said.

As soon as they were alone together, Anna Maria spoke sharply to Karen. "Are you really too ill to keep the child? She's still too young to be any use to me in Stockholm. I run a boarding school for girls. I really don't have time to look after Jenny. Oh! why was she ever born?"

"Because you loved her father," Karen said. "You did, didn't you?"

Anna Maria laughed bitterly. "I did. Oh, Niclas Lind was a charmer. When he sang, I forgot my troubles. But I didn't know that he was good for nothing but singing. And his kind of singing doesn't put bread in our mouths."

In a few minutes Carl and Jenny were back.

"I've tried to explain things to Jenny, Anna Maria," Carl said. "I think she'll go with you quietly now."

Anna Maria nodded. "Then we'll be off. Come, Jenny."

Carl gave Jenny a gentle push. "Go, child."

Jenny took a step forward. Then she whirled to look at Carl again. "But I can't! I haven't said good-bye to the boys."

"The boys are in school. We can't wait for them," Anna Maria said. She took Jenny's arm and pulled her along.

In the carriage Jenny cried stormily for a few minutes. Through her tears she watched the familiar sights go past. There were the garden and the little pond where she and the boys she called her brothers sailed boats. There was the small church where Carl Ferndal played the organ on Sundays.

"When will we be coming back?" she asked Anna Maria.

"Probably never," said Anna Maria. "You might as well know that right now. From now on, you're stuck with me and I'm stuck with you."

Carl Ferndal had warned Jenny that life in the city would be different from life in the country. He hadn't told her, though, that *she* must be different. She was used to running and singing and shouting. Now, no matter what she did, Anna Maria scolded her.

"How can such a tiny thing be so naughty?" Anna Maria said to Niclas Lind, on one of the rare evenings he spent at home.

"She's not naughty," Niclas answered. "She's just been spoiled by life in the country." He picked Jenny up and set her on his knee. "I've no doubt she misses the Ferndals, Anna Maria. Your cousin Carl's wife runs a much gayer household than you do, you know."

"She can afford to!" snapped Anna Maria. "Her husband has a good job. He doesn't spend his time in taverns, the way you do. I might be gay too, if I don't have to earn the bread that you eat!"

"Man can't live by bread alone," said Niclas.

For some weeks the only times Jenny was happy were when Niclas was home. Then, in late November 1823, her grandmother, Fru Tengmark, came for a visit.

Anna Maria was delighted. "You can take care of Jenny for me," she said to Fru Tengmark.

Fru Tengmark was a gentle, loving woman, whom Jenny liked at once. She was also a religious woman. She read the Bible regularly and went to church twice a week.

Jenny was glad to go to church again. She could sing there without being scolded.

"I love to sing, Grandmother," she said. "Do you think God likes to hear me?"

Fru Tengmark nodded. "I'm sure He does, child. He gave you your sweet voice. Be sure you never use it in a way that makes Him sorry He blessed you with it."

Fru Tengmark was a good influence for Jenny. Under her care Jenny learned to speak and to walk softly. In particular, she learned to be quiet during the hours her mother's school was in session.

Fru Lind had ten girl pupils. She taught them simple arithmetic and penmanship. She also taught them "ladylike" subjects such as French, embroidery, and china painting.

One spring day Jenny, who was almost four, was alone. She was looking idly out a window, wishing something interesting would happen. Suddenly a column of soldiers turned into the street. They were playing music. When they were close to Jenny's window, Jenny waved. As if saluting her in return, a bugler sounded a fanfare. Ta-ta-ra! Ta-ra-tata-ta-ta-ra!

Jenny clapped her hands. "Oh! I wish they'd play that again!"

But the band marched away.

"I'll have to play it myself!" Jenny said.

She hurried to the piano. She forgot she had been told not to touch it. She forgot about being still too. All she could think of was that lovely ta-ta-ra!

She put a finger on one key after another. Finally she heard one that sounded right. She continued until she had all the notes. Ta-ta-ra! Ta-ra-tata-ta-ta-ra!

She played the fanfare over and over, until she heard a voice calling. Then she remembered she wasn't supposed to touch the piano.

Quickly she ducked under it. Then footsteps approached and she held her breath.

"The piano didn't play by itself," her grandmother's voice said.

Jenny let out her breath with a little gasp. Fru Tengmark heard and bent down to look.

"Jenny! Was it you who played that tune?"

Jenny nodded. "Yes, Grandmother." And she crawled out from her hiding place.

"Praise be to God!" Fru Tengmark said.

"Then you aren't cross with me?" asked Jenny.

Her grandmother brushed the dust off Jenny's dress gently. "No, child."

But then Jenny's mother appeared. "What's going on here?" she demanded. "Jenny, have you been banging on my piano?"

Fru Tengmark answered for her.

"She has been playing, Anna Maria. Playing."

"How could she be? She's never had a lesson."

"She was, nevertheless."

"Then she can do it again," Fru Lind said. "So do it, Jenny. Now."

Jenny trembled, but she did it. The stirring fanfare sounded again. Ta-ta-ra! Ta-ra-tata-ta-ta-ra!

Now it was Fru Lind's turn to be amazed. "It's a miracle!" she said.

Fru Tengmark nodded. "You'll live to praise the day this child was born, Anna Maria," she said.

"I will, will I?" said Fru Lind. "Well, that day can't come soon enough for me. I need something to be thankful for in this miserable world!"

But she gave Jenny permission to play the piano if she wanted to, and that made Jenny very happy.

2 "You Sing Like an Angel"

It was lucky that Jenny had the piano to comfort her, because that August her grandmother left the Lind household and went to live in a Swedish Widows' Home. Fru Lind was too busy to take Jenny there to visit very often.

With Fru Tengmark gone there was now no one to look after Jenny during school hours. She had to sit in the classroom with her mother's pupils, who were all much older than she. There, if she so much as wiggled in her seat, her mother scolded her.

"Fold your hands in front of you and sit still!" Fru Lind said.

Things did not get any easier for Jenny in the next few years. Prices rose in Sweden and the cost of keeping a school rose too. Fru Lind had to charge her pupils more money. Some parents would not pay more and withdrew their daughters.

One night Jenny was lying awake in bed. She heard her mother speak fretfully to her father.

"If this keeps up, I won't have any pupils left. Then what will we do for money? What little you make, you spend."

"Eat, drink, and be merry!" said Niclas Lind. "For tomorrow, who knows? I may be dead!"

And he strummed a few notes on his guitar.

"Stop that!" Anna Maria said. "I want to speak seriously to you, for once."

"Not to me!" said Niclas.

He began to sing and Jenny listened happily. She even sang along with him, but softly, so she would not be heard. Anna Maria did not like to have her sing.

"I won't have you taking after your father,"
Fru Lind often said.

Jenny really sang now only when she was
with her grandmother at the Widows' Home.
All the old ladies loved to hear the little tunes
she made up. They liked to have her sing their
favorite hymns too.

"You sing like an angel, Jenny," they told her.

Early in 1828 only one boarding pupil remained
in Fru Lind's school. And she was already talking

of leaving. When she did Fru Lind would have to find some other means of making money.

"I could get a position as governess quickly enough," she told Jenny, "if I didn't have you to think about."

Then two things happened at almost the same time. The last boarder left, and Fru Lind saw an ad in the paper. It told her what to do with Jenny.

"I'm going to take a job in a town south of Stockholm," she told Jenny. "You'll go to live with a man and woman who want a child to care for."

Jenny was eight years old now, and she knew better than to make a fuss. All she said was, "What will Papa Niclas do?"

"Take care of himself," her mother answered.

Jenny could not help crying a little. When she sniffed, her mother made an almost affectionate gesture. She wiped Jenny's eyes with her own crisp handkerchief.

"You haven't asked me where you're going," Fru Lind said. "You'll live with the caretaker of the Widows' Home and his wife. You'll be able to see your grandmother every day."

The next year was very happy for Jenny. Her mother had constantly criticized her and called her "ugly little dwarf." At the Widows' Home, everyone complimented her and made a pet of her. She could sing and dance whenever she liked, and nobody scolded her at all.

Jenny's repertory of songs kept growing. She was attending church regularly again and there she learned new hymns. The old ladies, who came from all over Sweden, taught her their folk songs. She loved the simple tunes. Perhaps she still dimly remembered how happy she herself had been in the country.

A window of the caretaker's lodge faced the main street. Jenny liked to sit on the window sill and watch the traffic. Men and women strolled past. Lords and ladies rode by in carriages drawn by prancing horses. Soldiers marched to the parade ground in the King's park.

As Jenny watched she often sang. She sang anything that came into her head. Often she

imitated the sounds she heard: the tinkling of bells or the caroling of birds.

People passing by heard her, and sometimes they stopped to listen. If she was singing something familiar, they often continued on their way singing too. When this happened Jenny noticed and was pleased. Usually, though, she was unaware of her audience.

One day in August 1830, Fru Lind came for a visit. While she was at the lodge, a strange young woman knocked at the door. She curtsied to Fru Tengmark and Fru Lind and smiled at Jenny.

"I am maid to Mademoiselle Lundberg, solo dancer at the Royal Opera House," she said. "I have a message from her about the little girl."

Fru Lind frowned at Jenny. "What have you done now, Jenny?"

"Nothing wrong, Madam," the maid said quickly. "It's just that I've often heard the little girl sing. I told my mistress the child sings better than a lark. Now my mistress wants to hear her."

"Indeed," said Fru Lind. "What good will come to Jenny from that?"

"Why, who knows?" said the maid. "My mistress has influence at the Opera House."

"Humpf!" said Fru Lind. "And when does Mademoiselle want to see Jenny?"

"Tomorrow afternoon, Madam, any time between two and five."

After giving the address the maid curtsied again and departed.

"Will you take her?" Fru Tengmark asked Anna Maria.

Fru Lind shrugged. "I suppose it won't hurt Jenny to go to this person's apartment. It isn't as if I were taking her to the theater itself."

Jenny hung back shyly when she first saw the pretty dancer. Mademoiselle Lundberg talked to her quietly for a few moments before asking her to sing. By then Jenny was ready.

She sang several rollicking melodies while the dancer swayed in rhythm.

"Delightful!" Mademoiselle Lundberg said, when Jenny was finished. "She has as sweet and true a voice as I have ever heard. You must let her sing for the directors of the Royal Theater. I believe they will say she could be educated for the stage."

Fru Lind threw up her hands in horror. "The stage! Never! The theater is not a proper place for a young girl. Everybody knows that theater people lead immoral lives!"

The dancer looked as if she had been slapped. She kept her self-control, however, and replied calmly.

"But you can't let a voice like Jenny's go untrained, Madam. Please let me give you an introduction to Herr Croelius. He is the singing master of the Theater School, which is controlled by the Lord High Chamberlain."

The last words had a magical effect. The Lord Chamberlain was a high official at the royal court. And Fru Lind, like all loyal Swedes, thought that everybody connected with the royal family was above reproach.

"All right," she said. "I'll see about an appointment with Herr Croelius."

3 Actress-Pupil Jenny

The Theater School was in the Royal Opera House. Jenny had seen the Opera House before, but she had never been in it. Her mother believed that everything connected with the stage was evil.

"Stage performances are works of the devil," Fru Lind had often told the girls in her school.

Now, however, she and Jenny were actually walking up the broad steps of the handsome gray building. Jenny looked around uneasily. She was both afraid and excited at the thought of what she might see.

The Theater School was on the second floor. Herr Croelius was not ready to see them, so Jenny and her mother had to wait. Fru Lind sat on the edge of a hard bench and fretted.

"We shouldn't have come," she said. "This is no place for you, Jenny."

Before she could decide to leave, though, Herr Croelius appeared. He was fat and jolly looking. Jenny liked him at once.

He ushered them into his studio, and seated Fru Lind. Then he smiled at Jenny.

"Sing something, child," he said.

She sang an air from one of Peter von Winter's operas. When she had finished, Herr Croelius's eyes were wet with tears.

"Where did a child like you learn such an aria as that one?" he asked. "Not even Maria Malibran could sing it more sweetly."

Fru Lind smiled smugly. Malibran was the most famous opera singer of the day.

"I didn't even know I knew it," said Jenny. "I just hear something, and it sticks in my mind."

"Amazing!" said Herr Croelius. "Count Pucke must come listen to you. As head of the Royal Theater, he must share the pleasure with me."

He left the room. When he returned Count Pucke was with him. The Count, however, did not look a bit happy about seeing Jenny. He spoke in a low voice to Croelius, but Jenny heard what he said.

"What can you be thinking of, Croelius? She's not a bit pretty. She's very small and skinny and pale. A most unsuitable person for the theater!"

Poor Jenny wished she could sink through the floor. But Herr Croelius didn't look disturbed.

"Please, Count, just listen to her sing," he said.

"Oh, all right," said the Count. Then, to Jenny he said, "Sing something and be quick about it."

Jenny opened her mouth but no sound came out. Herr Croelius stepped forward and patted her shoulder gently.

"Please favor us with a song, Jenny. Anything you want to sing."

This time Jenny sang the folk tune *"Kom Hyra"* (Come Hither).

"Come hither, come hither,
      My pretty herd.
   Come cow, come calf,
      Come all my cattle dear!
   The sun is setting behind the hills,
      And shadows are lengthening.
   The night will soon close in.
      Come hither!"

The song was a favorite with Fru Tengmark's friends. It had a leaping melody and showed the full range of Jenny's voice.

The Count was silent for a moment after Jenny had finished. When he spoke again his voice trembled.

"It's a miracle!" he said. "When she sings she is transformed. Croelius, sign her up. We must train her for our theater!"

"Oh, no you won't!" said Fru Lind. "The theater is evil. Actors and actresses lead sinful lives. I won't sacrifice my daughter to the stage!"

Both Croelius and Count Pucke looked amazed.

"Why else did you bring her here?" asked Herr Croelius.

"To find out if she really has a good voice," Anna Maria replied. "Where else could I get such a reliable opinion, with no cost to myself?"

"Ah!" said Count Pucke.

He beckoned to Croelius and the two men went aside to talk. Then Croelius spoke again to Anna Maria.

"Madam," he said, "just think what else can

be had at no cost to yourself. Jenny can be educated and brought up entirely at the government's expense. She can receive lessons in singing, elocution, court French, and everything else suitable for the culture of a young woman."

Fru Lind sniffed. "And live in the theater atmosphere? You call that suitable?"

"There is no reason why she cannot live at home with you, Madam," Count Pucke said. "We will pay you for her keep."

"Well—" said Anna Maria.

"And," the Count added, "we will also pay you to board and keep three other pupils."

The last offer was too tempting for Anna Maria to refuse. "Very well," she said, "I accept those terms."

Jenny became an actress-pupil at the Theater School in September 1830, a month before her tenth birthday. There, all the regular school subjects were taught, but the emphasis was on the theater arts. These included dancing, singing, playing the piano, and acting. Jenny particularly enjoyed the acting.

The November following her entrance into the school, she was given a real part in a stage performance. It was unusual for a new pupil to have such a chance. She owed her good luck to the fact that she was so tiny. The scheduled play was *The Polish Mine*, a melodrama. One of the characters was supposed to be a seven-year-old girl. Jenny was the only pupil who looked that young.

"Aren't you scared?" the other girls asked her. "Aren't you afraid you'll forget what to do when you get on stage?"

"I don't think so," said Jenny.

But when the moment for her entrance came, she was frightened. Her legs shook and she felt very hot.

"I think I must be sick." she said to the director. "I can't go on!"

"Yes, you can," he assured her. "Go!"

So Jenny stepped out onto the stage — and the miracle happened. She became Angela, the girl who would do anything to get her mother out of the mine where she was imprisoned.

All her life afterwards, Jenny remembered the praise she received that night. She remembered happily the sound of the applause and the scent of the flowers the audience tossed at her feet. She remembered the heart-warming congratulations of her teachers and of the other girls.

But she remembered sadly the words of her mother. "I suppose your acting was good enough, but why didn't they let you sing? That's what they're supposed to be training you to do!"

The remark was typical of Anna Maria. She was never quite satisfied with anything. And, of course, she had always found fault with Jenny. Now she was equally disagreeable with the three other girls the directors had boarded with her. Finally one of those girls went to Mademoiselle Bayard, the school supervisor.

"We can't stand living with Fru Lind a day longer. Please put us somewhere else," the girl said.

Mademoiselle Bayard found rooms for them on the top floor of the Opera House. She herself became their chaperon.

Jenny often visited them there. She saw how happy they were and how they loved Mademoiselle Bayard.

"What fun you have together," she said wistfully.

"Come join us, then," they urged.

"I wish I could," said Jenny, "but I can't."

The wish was planted in Jenny's mind, though. Whenever Anna Maria was especially mean to her, the wish grew stronger. At last, after a particularly bitter fight with her mother, she asked Mademoiselle Bayard to accept her too. Jenny had just turned fourteen.

Permission had to come from the directors. By now they knew for themselves how difficult Fru Lind was. They allowed Jenny to move into the Opera House.

Fru Lind was furious. She demanded that Jenny be returned to her, but the directors refused.

"Read the contract we have with you," they told her. "We think you have failed to provide the 'tender loving care' it calls for from a chaperon."

Fru Lind was silenced by this accusation, and Jenny stayed at the Opera House. For a year and a half, she enjoyed a happy give-and-take life with the other girls. In the summer of 1835, they all went to a little inland lake on holiday. There Jenny delighted again in the simple pleasures she had known as a small girl with the Ferndals.

During this time away from her mother, Jenny

became a disciplined professional too. She appeared in eighteen different plays. She also made her first appearance in opera. It was one composed by Adolf Lindblad, the leading Swedish composer of the time.

Jenny's growing popularity did not escape Fru Lind's notice. Finally she decided to look up Niclas Lind and force him to demand Jenny's return home. Niclas took the matter to court. The judge decreed that, if her father wanted her, Jenny must live with him until she married.

The return home was not as bad as Jenny had feared. For one thing, her father was there too. For another, Anna Maria had been frightened by Jenny's flight. She made an effort to be kinder to Jenny. So the atmosphere in the Lind household was happier than before.

And so the years of Jenny's schooling passed. In January 1837, the directors placed her on a fixed salary as an actress. She was to receive 700 Riksdaler Banco (about $150) a year. She would also get some extra money every time she appeared on stage.

In 1837 Jenny appeared 92 times. She played a range from slapstick comedy to deep tragedy, from light operetta to grand opera. In December, at the age of seventeen, she was given a special "plum." She had the chance to introduce the music of a German composer, Jakob (Giacomo) Meyerbeer, to a Swedish audience.

In a scene from the opera *Robert le Diable* (Robert the Devil), Jenny sang the appealing role of Alice, Robert's human foster sister. It was better suited to her voice than any other part she had ever sung. The audience realized her skill in the role at once.

Jenny's official biographers, Holland and Rockstro, spoke of her singing of this role many years later:

> "The tradition still lives of the effect she produced on all who heard her. It was a short flight, in which she merely tried her wings. But it opened the way to flights that carried her far and wide."

One of Jenny's most popular roles was that of
Alice in *Robert le Diable*.

4 The Swedish Nightingale

The scene from *Robert le Diable* was repeated four times that December. The Swedish people continued to be enthusiastic about Jenny's singing of her brief role.

"We must hear Mademoiselle Lind in a full opera!" they said.

Isak Berg, who had become singing master after Herr Croelius's retirement, objected.

"She is too young—barely seventeen—for so heavy a task," he said.

However, he finally gave in to the public. Jenny was soon studying the role of Agathe in Weber's *Der Freischütz*. Jenny could scarcely believe her good luck. *Der Freischütz* was an important opera and a favorite with Stockholm theater-goers.

Her teacher was Madame Erikson, a former opera singer.

"Oh, Madame!" said Jenny. "Of all opera roles, I think Agathe is my favorite. Do you think I can do it well?"

"I think you will be able to," said Madame Erikson. "But first, my dear, you have a lot to learn."

"I know," said Jenny. "And I will practice very hard."

She did. She practiced so hard and such long hours that she grew very nervous.

"You must now practice being calm," Madame Erikson said. "We can't have your voice shaking when you sing Agathe's prayer."

The title *Der Freischütz* means "The Free-Shooter." According to an old German legend, he was a marksman who made a bargain with the Devil. The Devil would give him seven magic bullets. Each bullet would hit its mark, no matter how "freely" it was shot. But after the seventh shot, the marksman would belong to the Devil—unless a stronger power intervened before that bullet hit its mark.

In Weber's opera the free-shooter, named Max, is in love with Agathe. Agathe says she will marry him if he wins the Prince's shooting contest. To be sure of winning, Max bargains with the Devil. The seventh thing he is asked to shoot is a white dove. The dove is Agathe in disguise. She prays he will not shoot, but she is too late. She is wounded, but not fatally. Because she prayed the Lord heals her, and frees Max from his bargain with the Devil.

A few days before opening night, Jenny asked a favor of her teacher. "May I sing my part to you, Madame? You may have some criticism."

Jenny gave herself wholeheartedly to the role. When she finished, she looked questioningly at Madame Erikson. Tears were rolling down the teacher's face.

"Was I so bad?" Jenny asked sadly.

"Bad! My child, there are no words to tell you how glorious your voice is. From now on I have nothing more to teach you. Do as God directs you."

In spite of her teacher's praise, Jenny was sure she would fail miserably in the actual performance.

"Jenny, you'll be fine, as you always are," her friends told her.

"But I've never been the leading performer before," she said.

On March 7, 1838, the audience saw a thin, frightened girl walk on stage. She looked very ordinary. Her hair was parted in the middle with little bunches of curls on either side of her pale face. She was dressed in a peasant costume, and it did not become her. But then she opened her mouth—and suddenly she was not plain Jenny. She was Agathe. The people knew at once that she was the most memorable Agathe they had ever heard.

Jenny knew the evening had given her the most remarkable experience of her life. Before she went to bed, she fell on her knees and thanked God.

"This is my true birthday," she said. "I got up this morning one creature. I go to bed another. I have found my power."

The directors of the Royal Theater recognized the importance of the occasion too. They gave her two silver candlesticks engraved with the words: "In Remembrance of March 7th."

Jenny's triumph in *Der Freischütz* had come at a most welcome time. The older stars of the Swedish Royal Theater were fading, and the Swedish public was ready for some fresh, new

talent. The Swedes took Jenny to their hearts.

She sang the role of Agathe nine more times in 1838. She also sang 64 times in other roles. Everywhere she went people recognized her.

"It's Jenny Lind!" they would say, and press forward to touch her.

In June 1839 Jenny gave a concert in the university town of Uppsala. The students went wild with enthusiasm. After her performance they unhitched the horses from her carriage and pulled it through the streets themselves. When

she had gone to bed, they stood under her
window and serenaded her all night long.

"Come to me, thou who took my heart;
Come to me, beautiful rose of the
northern forest . . ."

The romantic song made the eighteen-year-old
girl wish she had someone to love.

She found him that same year. He was Julius
Günther, the handsome new tenor at the Royal
Opera. Unfortunately for Jenny he was the idol
of many beautiful Stockholm ladies. Thin, plain
little Jenny was nothing to him but a fellow
singer.

Fortunately for her, however, the Opera had
another new male singer, Giovanni Belletti. He
had a fine Italian baritone voice, but he was shy
and quiet. Jenny felt comfortable with him. He
soon became her "dear dependable friend."

Jenny had another dear friend too, Louise
Johansson. Louise had been a boarder at Anna
Maria's original school. Now she was a sales-

woman in a Stockholm shop. Jenny urged her to come and live with the Linds.

At first Anna Maria was delighted to have the extra income Louise brought and treated her kindly. Gradually, though, she began to complain about everything Louise did. Jenny always flew to her friend's defense. This made Fru Lind furious. Finally she screamed at both girls.

"If you don't like it here, leave!"

The girls left. They went to Jenny's Aunt Lona Lindskog's home. There Louise might find permanent refuge, but Jenny feared it would be only temporary for her.

She was right. The Linds found her there shortly. But this time they could not make a scene. In the first place Lona Lindskog was a relative. In the second place, Jenny was now nineteen, and too famous to be treated like a straying child.

Adolf Lindblad, the composer, was an admirer of Jenny's singing. When he heard of her problem, he invited her to come and live with his family.

With the Lindblads Jenny found what she afterwards called her "first real home." There she was loved and respected. There, too, she met everyone who was doing serious work in the arts. She heard the finest music and the best talk in Sweden.

Jenny was able to repay the Lindblads by helping Adolf with his songs. Her voice was the perfect instrument for them. She became his inspiration for writing others. She sang his songs at concerts and made them popular.

Jenny had moved to the Lindblads in December 1839. The following year was one of triumph for her. On January 1, 1840, the Royal Theater directors raised her salary by $50. On January 13th, she was appointed Court Singer by His Majesty, King Karl Johan. This was the highest official recognition possible in Sweden for a singer. Later in the year she was made a member of the Swedish Royal Academy of Music by unanimous choice of fellow musicians.

That spring Jenny went to Uppsala again. As before her voice charmed the audience. The music critic of the *Uppsala Correspondenten* wrote poetically about her: "In addition to Nature's beautiful songbirds, there came flying from Stockholm on Whitsun Eve a nobler nightingale: the famous Jenny Lind."

The comparison struck popular fancy. From that time on, Jenny was known as the "Swedish Nightingale."

5 "You Have No Voice Left"

One person whom Jenny had met at the Lindblads' was Erik Geijer. He was a history professor at Uppsala University and also a talented song composer. He had attended her second concert in Uppsala. Unlike the rest of the audience, though, he had not been entirely pleased with her.

"I do not want to alarm you, my dear," he said, "but your voice sounded a little strained to me. I suggest you ask your singing master how to control the stress of different notes."

Jenny had been disturbed herself because her vocal chords felt tired. After Geijer's warning, she went to see Isak Berg. He treated her fear lightly.

"All you need is a few days of rest," he said.

But Jenny was not satisfied with that diagnosis. She sought another opinion. She had always admired the seemingly effortless way her friend Belletti sang, so she consulted him.

"I, too, have been a little worried about your voice," he said. "But I do not think any teacher in Sweden can help you. In fact, there is only one person I know of who really understands voice production. He has made a study of throat and vocal chord structure."

"And who is he?" asked Jenny.

"Manuel García," Belletti said. "He has a studio in Paris."

"Then I will go to Paris to see what he can do to help me," said Jenny.

Before she could go, though, she had to earn money for the trip. She would have to support herself in Paris and pay for lessons as well.

The only way she knew how to make money was by singing. Therefore, even though her

Jenny's role in *Lucia di Lammermoor* was a difficult one for her tired voice.

voice needed a rest, she spent the summer of 1840 on a concert tour around Sweden. In the fall, without any vacation at all, she returned to Stockholm and a full opera season.

At the start she appeared as Lucia in *Lucia di Lammermoor*. The part required more vocal acrobatics than any other soprano role, and it severely taxed her already tired voice. Yet her audiences were blind to her difficulties. They called for encores time and again.

That season, too, she repeated her successes in *Robert le Diable* and *Der Freischütz*. To those popular roles she added a new one, that of the Druid priestess, Norma, in Bellini's opera of the same name.

In December, 1840, the directors approached Jenny with a new three-year contract. It offered her the highest salary within their power. It also allowed her to have the summers free.

Jenny was tempted to sign, but she knew she must not. She wrote the directors a long letter and told them she was going to Paris. She explained: "I hope to study there with Manuel García. Perhaps I will learn from him how to produce a better voice for you."

Jenny went to Paris with high hopes. She was eager to start lessons with García. But when she approached his house for her first interview, she felt jittery. She scolded herself.

"Calm down, Jenny Lind. All Sweden thinks your voice is glorious. Why shouldn't García?"

García received her kindly, but wasted no time in getting down to business.

"Sing scales, please," he said. "I want to test the range of your voice."

Jenny had not sung scales for a long time, but she did as he asked. He did not comment on the result. He just asked her to sing an air from *Lucia di Lammermoor.*

Jenny was grateful for that choice. She had sung Lucia 39 times in the past year. Each time she had been noisily applauded.

She began to sing with unusual confidence. But suddenly her voice wavered and cracked. Sweat broke out on her forehead. Knowing she could not continue, Jenny stumbled to a chair and bowed her head in misery.

García did not try to encourage her.

"You can see for yourself, young lady, that you have wasted my time and yours. No matter how good your voice may have been, it is ruined now. You have no voice left."

Tears poured down Jenny's cheeks. "Isn't there anything I can do?"

García studied her for a few moments. While he did she gained control of herself. She wiped her eyes and sat up straight.

"There is one thing you may try," García said finally. "Rest your voice completely for six weeks. Don't sing a note. Don't speak any more than you must. At the end of that time, if you have taken my advice, come back. I will listen to you once more."

"Thank you," said Jenny.

She left his presence calmer than she had entered it. During the moments he had studied her, she had remembered her grandmother's warning. "God gave you your voice. Never use it in a way that will make Him sorry He blessed you with it."

Fru Tengmark was dead now and probably would never know how Jenny had abused her gift. The loss of her voice was His punishment. But He was merciful. If she proved she was truly repentant, He would restore it to her.

Jenny spent the six weeks studying French and Italian and attending the opera and the theater. She knew both activities would prove valuable in her future career, if God permitted her to have one.

At the end of the rest period, García accepted her as a pupil.

Jenny was so happy she could have kissed him. She determined to do everything in her power to show him her gratitude.

March 7, 1842, was the fourth anniversary of Jenny's "second birthday." It could have been a sad day for her, but she would not let it be. She wrote cheerfully to her friends, who she was sure were thinking of her and wishing her well:

"My singing is getting on quite satis-
factorily. I rejoice heartily in my voice.
It is clear and sonorous, with more
firmness and much greater flexibility
than it had before. A great deal re-
mains to be done, but the worst is over.
García is satisfied with me!"

In May Jenny realized that she could learn
nothing more from García. Her voice had not
only recovered but was better than it had ever
been before.

Now Jenny had to decide on her next move.
She wanted to return to Stockholm. But her
place at the Royal Theater had been taken by
another pupil of Isak Berg's. Would there be
room for her there at all?

The royal directors agreed to make room,
but the terms they offered were not nearly so
good as the last time. Nevertheless, she wrote
and accepted them.

6 The Voice That God Gave Back

When Jenny returned to Stockholm, the Lindblads urged her to live with them again. She was grateful for their loving support, because she did not know how the opera-goers of Sweden would greet her return.

The debut of her "new" voice was set for October 10, 1842. Jenny chose to display it in the same role she had sung in her farewell performance over a year ago: Norma. The choice was a direct challenge to Stockholm music critics. Jenny wanted them to recognize and acknowledge the change that had taken place.

They did. "Never have the walls of the Royal Theater in Stockholm echoed to a more finished, more enchanting song than that of Lind's *Casta Diva* . . ." one of them wrote.

Said another:

"Jenny Lind enraptured her audiences before by the truthfulness and warmth and poetry of her performances, but her technical development was never very sure . . . . Now, however, she shows not only a soprano voice of great sonority and range, capable of adapting itself to every shade of expression, but also she has gained a technical command over it great enough to be regarded as unique in the history of the musical world."

After such extravagant praise Jenny became the darling of Stockholm all over again. The court in particular took great pleasure in her. One of the Queen's ladies-in-waiting described her with some wonderment: "Mademoiselle Lind is of faultless behaviour and reputation; her manners are pleasing and modest; without being pretty, she has an expression of purity and genius."

By January 1843, Jenny was 23 years old. She was in better favor at the Royal Opera House than ever. And when contract time came around again, she was able to make demands of the directors.

One demand was that she be granted a leave of absence each year from June 15th to October 1st. Once again she was acting on advice from Professor Geijer.

"You say God restored your voice to you. The least you can do is share it with as many of His people as possible," he had said.

"Outside of Stockholm, you mean?" she had asked.

"Outside of Stockholm, outside of Sweden, outside of Europe," he had replied.

Jenny's first such adventure took her to Linköping, 100 miles away. With her went Julius

Julius Günther

Günther, the young tenor whom she had grown to love before she went to Paris. At that time, he had not cared for her romantically. Now, however, things were different.

"When I embrace Jenny on stage, a thrill goes through me. I wish I could hold her forever . . ." Günther had written to his friend, the composer Jakob Josephson.

Josephson was at the university in Linköping, and Julius introduced Jenny to him. She learned that Josephson was trying to scrape up enough money to study in Germany.

"Julius and I will help!" Jenny wrote to him later. "We'll give a concert for your benefit!"

It was the first concert Jenny had ever given for charity. It set a pattern for the rest of her life.

From Linköping Jenny went for a vacation to Copenhagen, Denmark. There she visited the Bournonvilles, whom she had met at the home of the Lindblads.

Like the Lindblads the Bournonvilles kept "open house" for their creative friends. Among them was the writer, Hans Christian Andersen, whose fairy tales were very popular.

"I hope Copenhagen is to have the pleasure of hearing you sing, Fröken Lind," Andersen said to Jenny.

But Jenny was not yet ready to follow the second step of Geijer's advice. She shook her head.

"I am afraid, Herr Andersen, and that is the truth. Suppose I stood on the Copenhagen stage and was hissed! I should never get over it!"

Andersen was sensitive himself and understood. He said nothing more about it.

Shortly after that, though, August Bournonville told Jenny that all Copenhagen wanted to hear her famous rendering of the role of Alice in *Robert le Diable.*

"I told the directors of the Theater Royal that I was sure you'd be willing to sing there," he said.

"But I'm not!" cried Jenny. "I do not know Danish."

"Ah!" said Bournonville. "That will not matter. You can sing in Swedish. The two languages are so much alike, the audience will be able to understand you!"

Jenny burst into tears. "I cannot. I really cannot!"

Unlike Andersen, Bournonville argued.

"This is very embarrassing," he said. "You'll make me appear a fool at the Theater Royal, as the opera will have to be canceled."

Jenny's eyes flashed. "I came for a quiet visit with you. I didn't expect you to lay a trap for me."

Her words hurt Bournonville. "I will cancel the opera at once," he said coldly.

Jenny was immediately ashamed of her outburst. "I—I'll think about it," she said.

In the silence of the night, she prayed for guidance. In the morning she told Bournonville she would sing.

On September 10, 1843, Jenny stood in the wings of the Copenhagen Theater. She was more frightened than she had been when she first sang Alice six years before.

"I'm sure they won't like me," she worried. "They are used to their beautiful Johanne Luise Heiberg. And I'm so homely!"

But the Danish public loved her. At the end of the first act, even the director and all of the orchestra joined in a standing ovation for her. Long after the performance, people milled about the streets shouting, "Jenny Lind!"

Hans Andersen did more than love Jenny's voice. He fell in love with Jenny herself.

"She is so kind and beautiful," he said.

He was too shy at first to speak openly of his love. He let the stories he wrote at that time speak for him.

Hans Christian Andersen

A friend of Bournonville's had been too ill to attend Jenny's performance. She went to his home to sing for him alone. Bournonville was so sure her singing had hastened his friend's recovery that he called her "Angel of Mercy."

Having heard about that, Andersen soon had a new story. Its title was, *The Angel.*

His story *The Nightingale* was inspired by Jenny's visit to the sick man too. It told how a nightingale, by its beautiful song, had driven death away from the Emperor of China.

Jenny's heart was touched by Andersen's gentle, subtle love-making. Finally, Andersen took courage and asked her to marry him.

His proposal flustered Jenny, for she was in love with Günther. Not knowing how to handle the situation, she refused him bluntly. Her cold treatment inspired yet another story, *The Snow Queen.*

Andersen wrote: "She was delicately lovely, but all ice — glittering, dazzling ice. Yet her eyes shone like two bright stars, and there was no rest or peace in them."

Perhaps he hoped that he could melt Jenny's coldness and bring her rest and peace. Certainly he continued to worship her, though she offered him nothing but friendship. It was through his championing of her that she was first brought to world attention. He had many influential friends.

One such friend was the German composer Meyerbeer, whom Jenny had met in Paris. His operas were the rage of Europe. His newest commission was to write an opera for the dedication of the Berlin Opera House.

Giacomo Meyerbeer

Andersen went to Berlin to visit Meyerbeer in the summer of 1844. The two talked about Meyerbeer's plan.

"It's the most ambitious thing I've ever done," Meyerbeer said. "The trouble is, I don't know any soprano who is right for the leading role."

"Will it be a typical Meyerbeer role?" asked Andersen. "If so, I'll wager Jenny Lind would be ideal. She certainly is perfect as Alice in your *Robert le Diable*."

Meyerbeer looked thoughtful. "Jenny Lind," he said. "I heard her sing in Paris. She does have a beautiful voice. But this part will call for a great deal of acting as well."

"Oh, she can act!" Andersen insisted. "Why, in Copenhagen, people praised her acting as much as her singing!"

Meyerbeer clapped a hand on Andersen's shoulder. "I can see that the songbird from Sweden has completely enraptured you," he said. "But I wonder if, under the circumstances, your judgment can be 100 percent trusted."

Andersen understood and was not offended.

"Get another opinion, by all means," he said.

When a well-known dancer who was visiting Berlin agreed with Andersen, Meyerbeer at last gave in.

He invited Jenny to play the part of Vielka in his new opera, *Das Feldlager in Schlesian* (Camp in Silesia). It would be presented on the opening night at the new Berlin Opera House on December 7, 1844.

7 An Instant Friendship

Meyerbeer's offer came at a good time. Jenny needed something to lift her spirits. King Karl Johann had died, and the Swedish Royal Theater was closed for a period of mourning. Moreover, Julius Günther had not been very attentive lately. Also, Jenny's mother was again causing trouble. She felt that the money Jenny spent on charity ought to be given to her parents, instead.

For all these reasons Jenny felt it would do her good to get away from Stockholm. They were powerful enough to overcome her fear of appearing before a strange audience. She accepted Meyerbeer's invitation.

As soon as she had accepted, though, she began to worry about being able to learn German in such a short time. She confided her uneasiness in a letter to Meyerbeer. He, too, began to worry. Could she learn German well enough to do his new opera justice?

"Go to Dresden to study," he wrote her. "There you will hear the purest German. There, too, you can attend the opera and study the German singers."

Jenny arrived in Dresden on July 25, 1844. She expected to stay until she would be called to Berlin for rehearsals. However, on August 28 she was recalled to Stockholm. As Court Singer, she was commanded to sing at the coronation of the new king, Oskar I.

With a new king on the throne, the Royal Theater could reopen. Naturally, the Swedish people wanted their songbird to stay with them. The directors of the Theater offered her a contract that would insure her an income for life.

Jenny was greatly tempted to break her promise to Meyerbeer and sign the contract. She remembered how she dreaded singing to strange audiences. Why shouldn't she stay in Sweden, where she knew she was admired?

Her friends Geijer and Lindblad were shocked at the question.

"You can't let Meyerbeer down," they said. "If you do, you will regret it all your life."

Meanwhile, Meyerbeer had learned of Jenny's recall to Sweden. He feared her duties as Court Singer would keep her away from rehearsals in Berlin. He was afraid, in fact, for the successful debut of his opera.

"The occasion is too important to permit taking any chances at all," he told the other performers. "Therefore, I am going to ask Fräulein Leopoldine Tuczec to learn the role of Vielka." Fräulein Tuczec was a popular German singer.

In mid-October, 1844, Jenny arrived in Berlin. Meyerbeer was delighted that she would be

One of the most beautiful paintings of Jenny was
done by artist Edvard Magnus.

able to sing the role after all. He did not tell her that Fräulein Tuczec had been studying it.

Jenny, however, was uneasy about the ordeal that lay ahead. Moreover, she really did not know German very well yet. Meyerbeer tried to bolster up her confidence, and praised her voice to all his friends.

He was pleased when the Princess of Prussia invited Jenny to sing at a reception. Jenny appeared at the reception in her usual simple white gown. As always her hair was parted in the middle with side curls.

She was introduced to the Countess of Westmorland, the wife of the British Ambassador. The Countess was amazed to find Jenny so pale and thin and shy. When Meyerbeer came up to her the Countess said, "Surely you can't be serious when you say Jenny Lind is to star in your opera. Why she looks like an awkward country girl."

But then Jenny began to sing. The first bell-like notes rang pleasantly in the Countess's ears. Her eyes widened in startled wonder.

Later, she tried to tell how Jenny's performance had affected her.

> "The wonderful notes came ringing out.
> But over and above that was the wonderful transfiguration — no other word
> could apply — which came over her
> entire face and figure. Her face shone
> like that of an angel."

The enthusiasm of the Countess encouraged Meyerbeer to believe Jenny could make her Berlin debut in *Das Feldlager* as planned. Therefore, two weeks before opening night, he gave Fräulein Tuczec the news.

She was furious. She insisted the part was hers and that she had a right to sing it.

"If necessary, I will go to the King," she threatened. When Jenny heard of the fuss, she felt nothing but relief.

"Let Fräulein Tuczec sing!" she said. "She knows the part and the German people know and love her. Besides, I am not really sure enough of my German to interpret the words properly."

Word of her decision spread quickly. People did not know that Jenny was glad to be saved from appearing in the unfamiliar role. They thought her action was saintly. Naturally, they were now more than ever eager to hear her sing.

A week after the opening night performance at the Opera House, they got their wish. Jenny appeared in her favorite role, that of Norma.

The audience came prepared to love her, and Jenny knew it. Therefore, for once she didn't even feel nervous beforehand. And she was sensational. When she had sung the *"Casta Diva"* (Queen of Heaven) aria, the audience rose as one person to clap for an encore:

> "Queen of heaven, while thou art
> reigning
> Love upon us is still remaining,
> Clad in purity...
> Queen of Heaven, hallow'd be thy
> presence!"

Jenny repeated the words. But she changed the aria from the key of G, in which it had been written, to the key of F, which she liked better.

Ever since that night, all sopranos have sung the "Casta Diva" in the key of F.

Jenny appeared twice more in *Norma* before Christmas. Then, as if it were a Christmas present, she was given a six months' contract with the Berlin Royal Opera. It promised her double the money Sweden had offered!

Jenny was thrilled at this evidence that Germany loved her. The money was much more than she needed, so she at once arranged to give everything "extra" away. She sent a large part of it to her friend Jakob Josephson, so he could study in Italy.

During her stay in Berlin, Jenny was entertained by many people. She felt most at home in the house of Professor Wichmann, a sculptor. At the Wichmanns', Jenny met Felix Mendelssohn, a brilliant German musician. He had composed his first mature work, the Overture to *A Midsummer Night's Dream*, at seventeen and had

Felix Mendelssohn

recently founded the Leipzig Conservatory.

Mendelssohn and Jenny liked each other instantly. Jenny spoke of that meeting often in later life, "In the first five minutes, I knew that I had made a lifelong friend."

In her six months with the Berlin opera, Jenny sang many roles. After she was sure enough of her German, she even sang the role of Vielka in Meyerbeer's *Das Feldlager in Schlesien*. And she was much better in the part than Fräulein Tuczec had been.

One night, in between acts of that opera, Jenny was called to the box of the British ambassador. A stranger was sitting with Lord Westmorland. He was Alfred Bunn, manager of Drury Lane Theater, London. Mr. Bunn wanted Jenny to sing at Drury Lane during the 1845-46 season. He offered her very good terms. He also painted an alluring picture of London life for her.

Jenny didn't know what to do. She looked to the Ambassador for advice. He had not really listened to the terms of the contract. He only thought how wonderful it would be for England to hear the incomparable Nightingale.

"I think it will be to your profit if you sign with Mr. Bunn," he told her.

Believing he was giving her good advice, Jenny signed. Then she hurried backstage to be ready for the next act.

At first Jenny was happy about the contract, as Mr. Bunn had promised her a great deal of money. For some time she had been saying she wanted to leave the opera stage as soon as she could afford to. "I would like to sing for charity,

Alfred Bunn

for my friends, and for my own pleasure, and that's all," she said. After the English engagement, she should be able to do just that, she thought.

But then she began to worry. British people were cold and unfriendly to singers, she had heard. And she couldn't speak a word of English!

She had always been worried about singing outside Sweden, of course. But this time she worried until she was a nervous wreck. In this state she wrote a number of unwise letters to Mr. Bunn.

He finally agreed to cancel the contract if Jenny would give him £500 ($1250) forfeit money.

Jenny did not have £500 to spare. All extra money she had made she had already given away. She told that to Mr. Bunn, but he was not at all sympathetic. He could not force her to come to England, but he could and did threaten her. He said, "If you come to England to sing for anyone else, I'll see that you go to jail..."

8 A Pure Heart and a Pure Life

The trouble with Mr. Bunn upset Jenny terribly. She said, and believed, that she never wanted to sing anywhere but Stockholm or Berlin for the rest of her life.

She might have held to that belief, if it had not been for Mendelssohn.

He was the conductor of the Leipzig symphony orchestra. It gave concerts in the exquisite *Gewandhaus* (Craftman's Hall), an acoustically perfect auditorium. Mendelssohn invited Jenny to sing there in December 1845. She was under contract in Berlin at the time, but the director gave her permission to accept.

Ordinarily students at the Leipzig Conservatory were granted free tickets to Gewandhaus concerts. However, all Leipzig seemed willing to pay to hear Jenny. Therefore, free tickets were not issued for her concert.

The students were angry. They chose one of Mendelssohn's prize students, Otto Goldschmidt, to express their protest for them.

Goldschmidt could not get the ruling changed, but he was lucky enough to get a ticket for himself. He was also lucky enough to be introduced to Jenny.

Jenny was very cordial to the sixteen-year-old lad. Mendelssohn had told her about him, saying, "His father's rich as Croesus, but Otto will make his own mark in the world."

Jenny's looks disappointed Otto, but only until he heard her sing. Then, like nearly everybody who heard her, he was enchanted by the transformation that occurred.

"It is impossible to describe how Fräulein Lind

really looks," he said to his friends later. "When she sang the 'Casta Diva' she was the Queen of Heaven. When she sang Mendelssohn's 'Spring Song,' she was a dryad."

Jenny's first concert was so successful, she told Mendelssohn she would like to give a second.

"Only this time, I would like to give my share of the proceeds to the Gewandhaus Foundation," she said.

The Foundation provided funds for needy wid-

ows of former orchestra members. Mendelssohn was touched by the suggestion.

"All proceeds shall go to it," he promised.

After the second concert the Gewandhaus directors gave Jenny a silver tray, a present from the grateful musicians. Then she was serenaded by a group of students. Led by Otto Goldschmidt, they sang Mendelssohn's *"Waldlied"* (Forest Melody) to her.

Jenny was too overcome by the tribute to say

anything more than "Thank you all a thousand times."

After that evening Mendelssohn took every possible opportunity to work with Jenny. Like Lindblad he found inspiration in writing music for her voice. In composing his oratorio, *Elijah*, he filled the soprano solos with high F sharps.

"They are the loveliest notes she sings," he said.

For Jenny this friendship with Mendelssohn was the most wonderful thing she had ever known. Over and over she wrote of him in letters to Stockholm: "He is the dearest, kindest person in the world . . . He possesses the most supreme talent . . . In addition to everything else, he is so very personable!"

He was undoubtedly a man of great personal charm. But he was also a thoroughly good man.

Jenny grew to depend upon Mendelssohn's guidance. If he said she should do something, she did it without question. Also, she often followed his example in artistic matters. For instance, she had seen him help Clara Schumann,

Clara and Robert Schumann

the pianist. Later, she did the same for Clara's husband, the composer Robert. By adding some of Schumann's songs to her concert repertory, she made them popular.

When Mendelssohn told Jenny she should accept a new offer to sing in England, she agreed to do so.

Mr. Benjamin Lumley, manager of Her Majesty's Theater in London, wanted Jenny very badly. He was in trouble, because his singers were leaving him to sing at a newer and larger theater. He was prepared to do almost anything to get Jenny to sign a contract. But for a long time he had been urging her in vain. She was too afraid of the "wicked Mr. Bunn."

Lumley learned that Jenny was greatly influenced by Mendelssohn. When Mendelssohn was in England for a music festival in 1846, Lumley went to see him. Afterwards Mendelssohn wrote at length to Jenny.

He gave her all the reasons why she would be wise to accept Lumley's offer. Among them was the manager's promise to pay off her £500 forfeit to Mr. Bunn. Mendelssohn finished his letter by saying:

"I believe you will remember your visit here with pleasure all your life. I assure you the English people will receive you warmly. I believe there are no people more friendly, more cordial, or more constant. They will feel this way not only about your singing, but about yourself."

The 1847 season at Her Majesty's Theater in London opened on February 16. Jenny Lind was among the sopranos listed as due to appear. The opera scheduled for her debut was her old favorite, *Robert le Diable.*

But February passed, and March. Jenny still had not come to London. She was, in fact, having the worst attack of stage fright ever.

On April 16th she finally did arrive. But she still could not bear the thought of facing a British audience. Mr. Lumley was almost sick with worry over her indecision. At last she agreed to start rehearsals.

On the evening of May 4th, an enormous crowd filled the streets near Her Majesty's Theater. Everybody who could buy a ticket bought one.

When Jenny made her entrance as Alice, the audience rose and applauded her. After she had sung only a few bars of her first song, she was interrupted by frantic shouts of *"Brava! Brava!"* When the curtain fell after the final act, she was called forward again and again. Queen Victoria threw her own bouquet at Jenny's feet.

London went wild about Jenny and the enthusiasm spread through the British empire. Her picture appeared in every possible place: on candy boxes, match boxes, handkerchiefs, and chinaware.

Jenny made first appearances in several operas. *La Somnambula* (The Sleepwalker), *The Magic Flute*, and *Daughter of the Regiment* were among them. *La Somnambula* quickly became one of Queen Victoria's favorites. The part of Amina seemed to her perfect for the "angelic Jenny." "That exquisite shake, that wonderful

This cartoon in the English publication *Punch* was titled "Ye Publick—Its Excitement on Ye Appearance of Miss Lind."

clear, sweet *pianissimo* way of singing the very highest tones without losing any of their fullness and freshness! Oh, it's so wonderful!" Queen Victoria said.

By command of Her Majesty, Jenny sang twice at Buckingham Palace. She also sang at the new Royal Summer Palace on the Isle of Wight.

For the summer concert Jenny chose her favorite Swedish songs, four songs by Mendelssohn, and two from Mozart's *Marriage of Figaro*. When the concert was over, the Queen gave Jenny a jeweled bracelet. Then the two women talked together as friends. At that time Jenny told the Queen how much she wanted to leave the opera stage.

"It is such an artificial, unnatural life," Jenny said. "And there is so much rivalry among the actors. Christian charity is almost unknown among them."

"But, Miss Lind!" protested the Queen. "Do you not think of the loss this will be to art? I cannot bear to think of not hearing you sing any more!"

"Oh, I would continue to sing for my friends, Your Majesty," Jenny assured her.

After Jenny's contract in London had been fulfilled, she set out on a concert tour through the rest of England. Every fourth time she sang, she set aside the money for charity.

In November 1847 Jenny returned to Sweden for a visit. Almost at once she received the most heart-breaking news.

Mendelssohn was dead at the age of 38.

Jenny was bowed down by her grief. She could not bear to hear his name spoken. She could not sing his songs. Fortunately she had always taken comfort in religion. Now she went to church more frequently than before.

Also, there was work to be done. She gave a great many concerts for worthy causes. Then, when the opera season began, she sang again at the Swedish Royal Opera opposite Julius Günther.

That winter the tenor formally asked Jenny to marry him. She agreed, and they exchanged engagement rings.

Friends who knew them both shook their heads.

"It's too late for them," these friends said. "They have taken different paths too often."

Jenny was 27 now. She would have liked to retire at once and just be Julius's wife. But she had promised to return for another season in London. She kept that promise.

From London she sent Günther a watch.

"This will mark the time until we can be together again," she wrote on the accompanying card.

9 Angel of Charity

Jenny's second season in England was more triumphant than her first. She sang all the roles the English people had loved before. She added that of Lucia in *Lucia di Lammermoor* and of Elvira in *I Puritani* (The Puritans).

Her private life did not go smoothly, though. She wrote Günther that she lived for the season's end, so she could retire and just be his wife. He replied that he counted on her return to the Swedish Theater. They could star together there for years and years.

Trying to push from her thoughts her unhappiness over this idea, Jenny worked harder than ever for charitable causes. She gave benefit performances for hospitals. She gave money to needy musicians. She also helped young musicians to become known.

One such young musician was Otto Goldschmidt. She knew how much Mendelssohn had thought of his talent. She invited Otto to play two piano solos of his own choosing at one of her concerts. When he played Mendelssohn's "Songs Without Words," she burst into tears.

She was close to tears much of the time anyway. By now she realized that Günther's love for her was selfish. On the 26th of September, 1848, she wrote telling a friend in Sweden that the romance was over.

Otto Goldschmidt's playing of Mendelssohn's songs had showed Jenny how much she had missed hearing them. She learned that Otto and other friends of Mendelssohn wanted to set up a musical foundation in his name. She suggested a performance of his oratorio, *Elijah*, to start the fund-raising. The soprano solos had been written for her, but she had never sung them.

She appeared in *Elijah* at Exeter Hall, London, in December 1848. Singing this oratorio was the most soul-satisfying experience she had ever known. Oratorios derived their name from musical services that had been performed in the oratory, or prayer-chapel, of St. Philip Neri in Rome. All the time she was singing, Jenny felt as if she were praising God. She wished she need never again sing anything but the religious music she loved.

Crowds flocked to see Jenny at Exeter Hall.

She had to, though. She had promised Mr. Lumley that she would give six more operatic performances.

They topped everything that had gone before. When she appeared in the sixth and final performance, the audience both cheered and wept.

That night Jenny made a last entry in her opera book. She had begun it on her "second birthday"—March 7, 1838. She ended it on May 10, 1849.

In those eleven years she had given 677 performances in 30 different operas. The role of Alice in *Robert le Diable* had been her first operatic part. It was also her last. Jenny never sang in opera again.

In the fall she began a concert tour through Germany. She took Otto Goldschmidt with her as her accompanist. He seemed to know exactly how to make use of the piano to provide the right tonal background for her voice.

It was in Lübeck that John Hall Wilton caught up with her.

He had been sent from the United States by

the "Great Showman," Phineas T. Barnum. Barnum had first become famous for his humbuggery. That is, he pretended that things were what they were not — and he discovered that people loved being fooled. In his Great American Museum he exhibited a "Feejee Maid." Her upper part was a stuffed monkey, her lower part the tail of a big fish. He also showed a "Zip — the What Is It?" another make-believe monster.

In 1842 Barnum took a step away from humbuggery. He put a live midget on display. Calling his tiny man "General Tom Thumb," Barnum showed him all over the world. Queen Victoria even invited him to Buckingham Palace.

Now, five years later, Barnum wanted to take a giant step away. He wanted to show something or somebody that was not "odd" at all. Of course, whatever it was had to be the best of its kind in the world.

All reports told him Jenny Lind was "The Musical Wonder of the World." He engaged Mr. Wilton to find her and offer her a contract for 150 concerts.

The offer was very good, but Jenny hesitated. She was a little afraid of the way Barnum would "show" her. She wanted to be accepted for what she was, not for what someone said she was.

However, she did have a new charitable idea. She wanted to endow as many musical scholarships in Sweden as possible. And so she finally decided to accept Barnum's offer.

Barnum began "feeding" the newspapers in America with stories about Jenny's good works. He had pictures of his "Angel of Charity" put in shop windows. He made sure that sheet music of his "Singing Angel's" favorite songs was for

P. T. Barnum

sale everywhere. And he set up a song contest. He offered $200 to the writer of the best "Greeting to America" song for Jenny to sing.

If Jenny had known about any of this, she might have refused to go to the United States at all. But she didn't, and on Sunday, September 1, 1850, she arrived in New York.

Her welcome began the moment her ship was sighted. A two-gun salute was fired and a flag went up at the telegraph station on Staten Island. This was a signal for Barnum, who was waiting there with the port health officer. The two men jumped into a little boat and went out to the *S.S. Atlantic.* Barnum had to climb the ship's ladder one-handed. In the other hand he clutched a huge bouquet for Jenny.

Jenny and Barnum stood side by side as the ship nosed toward the pier. Thousands of people shouted and cheered from other ships anchored nearby. The pier was jammed with 30,000 other people. It was a colorful occasion, too, with American flags blowing in the wind, and red, white, and blue streamers.

Barnum's advance advertising of Jenny's arrival
in New York was a triumph of showmanship.

Jenny walked down the *Atlantic's* gangplank
on the captain's arm. Behind them walked
Barnum and the musicians Jenny had brought
with her: the conductor, Julius Benedict, and
the baritone, Giovanni Belletti. Following them
came Jenny's "lady companion," Josephine
Åhmansson, and her secretary, Max Hjortzberg.

Barnum's carriage was waiting for them. The
visitors got into it. Barnum himself climbed to
the driver's seat.

A crowd of people ran alongside the carriage. More than 200 bouquets were tossed through the windows to Jenny. When she arrived at the hotel, police had to clear a path for her so that she could enter the building.

Jenny smiled and waved bravely, but she felt terribly frightened. She wanted only to be alone and to rest.

Rest was impossible. The crowds in the street grew bigger with every passing hour. At midnight, 300 red-shirted firemen carrying flaming torches appeared. Behind them was a 200-member band, representing the Musical Fund Society.

"Miss Lind," Barnum said, "you really must greet these people."

He took her arm and led her out onto the balcony. She waved her hand and bowed as she had seen Queen Victoria do. For the next hour she was serenaded with patriotic tunes: "Hail Columbia," "Yankee Doodle," and others.

The next day, Monday, was equally frantic. The mayor and other celebrities called on her.

Leading hat shops, glove shops, and dressmakers sent her gifts from their wares. Reporters fired questions at her. Their newspapers printed every detail of Jenny's appearance.

That same day, Jenny, Barnum, Benedict, and Belletti set out to look at concert halls. They visited many. Finally they settled on Castle Garden.

It was the largest opera house in the nation. It was set on an island 200 feet beyond Battery Park at the foot of Manhattan island. A wooden

Jenny's first performance in America was held in New York City's Castle Garden.

bridge connected the island to the mainland.

Rehearsals began the next day. Barnum invited music critics to attend them. They were thrilled with Jenny's voice and praised "The Songbird from Sweden" in their newspapers.

Four days before opening night, Barnum held a ticket auction. Three thousand people braved a rainstorm to bid for the first ticket. It went to the owner of a man's hat store for $225! In no time at all every ticket was sold. The total amount collected was $17,864.

When Jenny heard the sum she was shocked. According to her contract, she was to receive $1000 a performance plus a half of all money taken in beyond $5000. That meant that from her debut alone she would get over $6000!

"It is wrong to make so much money so easily," she said. "It is taken from the American people. Therefore, I shall give my entire share of this first concert back to them."

This decision astonished Barnum, but he was delighted. Naturally, he spread the news. Interest in Jenny grew more feverish than ever.

10 Jenny in America

On opening night, Barnum proved what a "Great Showman" he was. He had an "Angel" to display. She must have a setting worthy of her. He made all arrangements with that end in mind.

Officials of the city cooperated. The chief of police with 60 of his men formed a double row from the door of Castle Garden across the bridge to the Battery grounds. Other police directed one-way traffic.

The doors were opened at five o'clock for the eight o'clock concert. Only a few guests were allowed on the bridge at once. But by performance time the huge audience was seated and waiting.

The people had plenty to look at. The souvenir program was 28 pages thick. The front cover carried pictures of Jenny, Benedict, and Belletti. Inside were details of their lives and careers, as well as complete program notes.

Jenny was not the first performer. Benedict conducted a specially selected 60-piece orchestra in the Overture to Weber's *Oberon*. Next Belletti sang a solo from Rossini's *Mahomet the Prophet*.

Then there was a pause, while Benedict left the conductor's stand and went backstage. When he reappeared he was escorting Jenny.

She was dressed all in white, except for a blue ribbon-belt. She wore no makeup, and her face was almost as white as her dress. When she saw the enormous crowd, she began to tremble. Benedict gave her hand a little squeeze, and she curtsied to the audience.

Every seat was filled for Jenny's first performance
in Castle Garden, September 11, 1850.

The gesture broke the spell for the people.
According to the New York *Tribune's* critic:

"It is impossible to describe the
spontaneous burst of welcome which
greeted her then. The vast assembly
rose as one man. For some minutes
nothing could be seen but the waving
of hands and handkerchiefs, nothing
heard but a storm of cheers."

For her first number Jenny had chosen her favorite aria, the "Casta Diva." Of that the *Tribune's* critic wrote too: "Every soprano has sung "Casta Diva" for us; but everyone else has seemed only trying to make music of it. Jenny Lind was the music."

Jenny sang duets with Belletti and some of her beloved Swedish folk songs. Of these the Herdsman's Song, *"Kom Hyra,"* was a resounding favorite with the listeners. They insisted on hearing it a second time.

In conclusion Jenny sang the tune that had won Barnum's contest. It was Bayard Taylor's "Greeting to America."

The entire evening was a stupendous success from every point of view. In commemoration of it Barnum had a Jenny Lind Medal made. One side of it showed Jenny's head in profile. On the other side were the details: place, date, attendance, even the amount Jenny made and gave to charity. The medals were sold by the thousands in hotel lobbies, by sidewalk vendors, and at newsstands.

After three weeks in New York, Jenny and her company went on tour. Everywhere they went Barnum's press agents had been first. Every town gave her a reception much like the one she had received in New York. Jenny began to grow very tired of being constantly on display.

So did other members of her company. At the end of the first tour, Julius Benedict had all he was willing to take.

"No more circus treatment for me," he said. "I shall return to England as soon as you find a replacement for me."

Julius Benedict was a pianist and composer as well as a musical director.

Benedict's assistant, Joseph Burke, was a good-enough conductor, but he was not a pianist, as Benedict was. Therefore, Jenny would need an accompanist. She sent to Europe for Otto Goldschmidt.

She knew Otto would come. At the age of 21, he would welcome the opportunity to play in America.

During her second stay in New York, Jenny was scheduled for fourteen concerts. After the seventh she told Barnum she wanted to buy her contract from him. Like Benedict, she had become tired of being displayed like a circus act.

"Our agreement says you may do so after you have given 100 concerts for me," Barnum said. "So far, you have given only 85 concerts. However, I will think about it."

He did, and he finally agreed. He was tired of dealing with temperamental musicians. Besides, he felt sure Jenny would soon see she could not succeed in America without him. After her ninety-third concert, they parted.

Almost at once, she realized that Barnum had

White dresses such as Jenny wore at Castle Garden became the rage in women's fashion.

given her much more than "circus treatment." He had left her free as the songbird she was called, by taking all business details on himself.

For a short time she tried to handle her own affairs, but she had no head for business. Besides, the effort left her with no strength to sing.

She went to a lawyer for advice. He recommended a Charles Seyton as business manager. Seyton took the job, agreeing to accept 25 percent of the receipts for his pay.

Thinking to increase his "take," Seyton began at once to pinch pennies. He did away with the attractive souvenir programs. He did nothing about arousing public interest.

The magic of Jenny's name still drew people who were aware she was in town. However, as Barnum well knew, the American public liked a "show." "Art for art's sake" did not satisfy them.

Before long attendance at Jenny's concerts grew less. So, consequently, did the box-office receipts. Seyton said the company could no longer afford to take a full orchestra on tour. Soon he did away with the orchestra altogether.

Such was the state of affairs when Otto Goldschmidt arrived. The whole burden of instrumental music was on him. He was a fine pianist, but he had no "feel" for what the American public wanted to hear. He played only what pleased him.

Jenny was very fond of Otto. In many ways he reminded her of Mendelssohn. Like him, Otto had dark romantic looks. Like Mendelssohn, too, he was gentle and sensitive. He was also very talented, and Jenny was determined to make the audiences accept him.

She did everything she could to push him to the forefront. She had his name printed in type as large as her own. She gave him a greater share of every concert. She even led applause from the wings for him, if it did not arise spontaneously.

She succeeded only in hurting her own "image" and embarrassing Otto. Finally, he voiced his feelings.

"Fräulein Lind, I would like to resign and return to Germany," he said. "I cannot impose on your kindness any longer. My presence here does not help you; it makes matters worse. I cannot bear the thought of hurting you in any way!"

Jenny was dreadfully upset. "But I need you, Otto," she said.

"Of course I won't leave until you find another accompanist," he assured her.

That wasn't the answer Jenny wanted, but she didn't know how to make him change his mind. Feeling quite desperate, she went to the baritone Belletti for advice.

"Isn't there something I can do?" she asked him.

"Stop treating him like a child," Belletti said bluntly. "Can't you see that Otto is in love with you, Jenny? Naturally, he wants you to think of him as a man!"

Jenny could hardly believe that Otto was in love with her. Why, she was 31! Nine years older than he!

Now that she knew he was in love with her, though, she realized she should have guessed it. Otto trembled when she touched him. He turned red when she complimented him.

She did not even try to find a substitute for him. He stayed on as he had promised. Soon Jenny had to admit that what she felt for him was love too. Knowing that he would never speak without her encouragement, she let him realize her feeling. Finally he got up the courage to propose to her.

"Fräulein," he said, "could you consider marrying me?"

"If you will promise to love, honor, and protect me, I will," she answered. Then she added, "Now that we are engaged, I really think you should call me Jenny!"

On February 5, 1852, Jenny and Otto were quietly married in Boston. As soon as the news got out, it was rushed to the telegraph offices and flashed to the far corners of the world.

The romance made Jenny popular again. People in the New England cities flocked to see the newlyweds. Otto and Jenny were so happy, they thought of making their home in New Hampshire or Massachusetts.

Then a letter came that changed their thinking. Otto was offered the position of professor of music at the Dresden Conservatory of Music. This was high recognition of her husband's talents, and Jenny was thrilled and delighted.

From that moment on, she declared, she would add his name to hers even in her professional life. Henceforth she was Madame Jenny Lind-Goldschmidt. And she didn't want anyone to forget it!

11 Return to Europe

Jenny's last American concerts were given in New York. They were not well attended. New Yorkers in general were not "romantics" like the citizens of other cities. They felt their "Angel" had lowered herself by marrying a mere man.

The real music lovers turned out to hear Jenny, but they too were disappointed. The programs offered too little variety. Jenny always sang an Italian aria (from *Norma, Lucia di Lammermoor,* or *La Somnambula*). She also sang songs by Mendelssohn or Schumann, an old

English ballad or two, and a Swedish song to finish.

The comments by the New York *Herald* had a special sting:

> "She sings pieces from operas and snatches of this and that, more in the clap-trap style than in accordance with the rigid rules of classical music. When she returns to Europe, she will have to prune away a great deal of the redundancies in which she indulged during her stay in this country."

In other words, the critic believed that Jenny was not giving her best to the American public.

The criticism hurt Jenny, but she had to admit that it was justified. Her repertory was limited. Also, after such a long tour, her voice was tired.

Her final American concert was held in Castle Garden. It was in sad contrast to her first one there. The great hall was only half-filled. There was no need at all for police protection.

Barnum was in the audience that night. After the performance he went to Jenny's dressing room to say good-bye. He found her in very low spirits.

"I shall not sing much in public any more, Mr. Barnum," she told him. "Perhaps, indeed, this has been my last public appearance. I am thankful to say I have all the money I will ever need."

"You must not say that," Barnum replied. "God has given you a voice beyond all others. People are willing to pay dearly to hear it. If you no longer need money for yourself, you can give it to the people who do."

Jenny was touched by the reminder. "Ah, Mr. Barnum, that is so true. And it would be very ungrateful of me not to use the gift of Our Heavenly Father for the benefit of the poor. I renew my pledge to do so. I shall continue to sing as long as my voice lasts."

Jenny was scheduled to depart on May 29, 1852. In comparison to her arrival, her leaving was very quiet. Only a small crowd turned up at the foot of Canal Street to wish her farewell. But at the last minute, 300 volunteer firemen, for whom Jenny had given a benefit, came to swell the number. They gave her a 7-x-3-inch gold box to remember them by.

She thanked them with tears in her eyes. "It is a gift worthy of royalty," she said. "I will cherish it always."

She stood at the rail as the ship backed away

from the pier. She looked with mixed feelings at the shores of America. There she had known great triumph and great despair. There, too, she had found her anchor for the rest of her life: her beloved husband, Otto Goldschmidt.

She would always be grateful to Barnum for making the visit possible.

For some months after her return to Europe, Jenny did nothing with music except sing pri-

vately for Otto and their friends. She had longed for love and a home, and now she had both. Her admiration and respect for Otto grew stronger every day. She wrote of her happiness to her friend Jakob Josephson, who had worked with Otto in Leipzig.

> "Otto is everything that a woman could ask of a man. He grows more lovable and devoted every day, in a most touching way. I, who was ill-schooled in many respects, benefit from his magnificent schooling. In music, I hear nothing from him but the greatest and finest."

Jenny had not forgotten the project that had sent her to America in the first place. She set up perpetual music scholarships at the universities in Uppsala and in Lund. From the beginning she took a strong interest in the young people who received those scholarships. She sent them letters of advice. She scolded

Jenny's tastes in fashion and hair styles were always simple and in good taste.

them in a motherly way if they did not seem to be working as hard as they should.

In September 1853 Jenny became the mother of a son, Walter Otto. She considered this another proof of God's great goodness. More than ever before, she felt she had to tell Him so in song.

Fortunately her companion on the American tour, Josephine Åhmansson, had stayed on with the Goldschmidts as their housekeeper. She made an admirable "second mother" for Walter. Jenny felt perfectly comfortable about leaving her son in Josephine's care.

Soon after his birth, therefore, Jenny started a series of oratorio concerts in large German cities. Her husband, Otto, accompanied her.

Her favorite oratorios were Mendelssohn's *Elijah,* Handel's *Messiah,* and Haydn's *The Creation.*

The Norwegian composer, Halfden Kjerulf, heard Jenny sing *The Creation.* He commented: "I wept from her first note to her last in Gabriel's aria. It was completely natural, sincerely simple, a wonderful beauty of sound."

Jenny sang *The Creation* in Halle, the birthplace of Haydn. She gave the concert to raise funds for a statue the townspeople wished to erect in his honor. She sang so movingly that the conductor, Robert Franz, lost his place in his score. The chorus and orchestra had to conduct itself until he found the place again.

The famous composer Johannes Brahms was in the audience that day. Years later he said: "Whenever I open the score of *The Creation,* the parts that were sung by Jenny Lind shine out as though printed in gold."

In 1855 Jenny gave concerts all over Holland. In 1856 she toured England, Scotland, and Wales. Her conductor in the British Isles was Julius Benedict, who had been in America with her. Of the British tour Benedict wrote in a letter to Joseph Burke: "The receipts for these concerts can only be compared to the best in the United States. Instead of waning, interest in Madame Lind-Goldschmidt is on the increase."

One of Jenny's greatest supporters in England had always been Queen Victoria. Now that Jenny was happily married, Victoria began to treat her as an intimate friend. The Queen, in fact, urged Jenny to make England her home.

Jenny was not ready to consider doing that. Otto wanted to return to Dresden and resume his teaching. What he wanted, she wanted too.

The Goldschmidts' second child, another Jenny, was born in March 1857. At the christening of the child, Jenny told the minister, "I thought my heart had all it could desire before, but now I must repeat it with even fuller meaning."

A year after the birth of little Jenny, the

Ernst, youngest of the Goldschmidt children, poses stiffly with sister Jenny.

Goldschmidts did move to England. Otto had decided he wanted to devote more time to composing music, and England was as good a place as any for that. They rented a house not far from Buckingham Palace, and were constant visitors both there and at Windsor Castle.

Otto was making a real name for himself now. He was responsible for what Queen Victoria called "The Great Musical Event of 1863." He revived two almost-forgotten works by Handel, the music to John Milton's poems *Allegro* and *Il Penseroso*. They were presented in St. James Hall, London. Fifty years had passed since their last presentation.

After Otto's success with the "forgotten Handel" he was offered the position of professor of piano at the Royal Academy of Music in London.

Jenny was delighted. "Now people will have to stop calling him 'Jenny's Prince Consort,'" she said.

Jenny loved Queen Victoria, but she felt a little sorry for her husband, Prince Albert. She wanted it clearly understood that in the Goldschmidt household Otto was king.

12 Last Performance

Otto was a good business manager. He knew how to use money to make money. He invested Jenny's funds so wisely that she had more and more to give to charity. In 1862 she was able to endow another full musical scholarship for young Swedes.

Jenny seldom went off on singing tours now, but she continued to use her voice for worthy causes. It was not so clear and true as it had once been, but her public didn't seem to care. People still flocked to hear her.

Jenny spent as much time at home as possible. A third child, Ernst, had been born in 1861, when Jenny was 41. Together with Josephine Åhmansson there were six in the family.

In 1864 the Goldschmidts built a home overlooking Wimbledon Park. Otto named it "Oak Lea" because of the many old oak trees that shaded the house.

The Goldschmidt home became the same kind of artistic center as the Lindblads' in Stockholm and the Bournonvilles' in Copenhagen. Artists and writers as well as musicians were always welcome there. Oak Lea was full of good talk and good music each day and far into the night.

Jenny loved nothing better than to gather family and friends around her at the piano. They sang the old folk tunes of Sweden. They sang the songs of Lindblad, Mendelssohn, and Schumann. Those who were privileged to sing informally with Jenny were thrilled by the experience. Among them was the Countess of Westmorland, who recorded her feeling: "In the peace of her home, Jenny's voice had a

quality of beauty I have never heard surpassed."

Perhaps this was so because of Jenny's great happiness there. She enjoyed the give-and-take of family life that she had never known as a child. She loved to fuss in the kitchen with little Jenny, letting the Swedish cook teach them both how to make good Swedish dishes. She delighted in listening to Walter's piano practice and in guiding Ernst's first attempts to read.

Otto was very busy. In 1866 he was made vice-principal of the Royal Academy of Music. He was still composing in what free time he had. In 1867 he finally completed the oratorio *Ruth,* based on the Bible story. He had composed the title role for Jenny's voice. She sang it in Exeter Hall and, in spite of her 47 years, sang gloriously.

In October 1870 Jenny became 50 years old. She knew that she should think about retiring altogether.

"Fifty is very advanced for a coloratura soprano," she said.

She did sing in public less and less often. But she sang for Queen Victoria whenever her friend "gently commanded."

In 1874 the Goldschmidts left their home in Wimbledon and moved to London. Otto's professional star was rising as Jenny's was falling. He was collecting all possible honors open to a musician in England. He became a member of the Royal College of Organists, the London Company of Musicians, and the Royal College of Music.

Queen Victoria of England.

And Queen Victoria chose him as the teacher to give piano lessons to her daughter, Princess Helena. The Princess came to the Goldschmidts' home for her lessons.

Their home was more than ever a musical center now that it was in London. Otto had a special group of amateur musicians meet with him there once a week. They called themselves the "Madrigal Society." They met to sing the works of neglected or "forgotten" composers.

One such "forgotten" composer at the time was Johann Sebastian Bach. One such "forgotten" work was his marvelous B Minor Mass. It had never been produced in England. Few people there had ever heard of it. Jenny herself had not.

"To think that an old woman like me, who has lived with music all her life, should be told of this music by an amateur!" she said.

Otto echoed her words. "We must see that it is produced in London," he added.

All that winter of 1876, the Madrigal Society studied and rehearsed the music. More singers had to be enlisted. Finally there were too many for the Goldschmidts' drawing-room. Rehearsals had to be moved to a public hall.

Jenny trained other singers for the soprano solo parts. She herself would agree only to lead the soprano section of the chorus.

The Bach B Minor Mass was performed for the first time in England on April 26, 1876. The handful of singers who had met just for fun in the Goldschmidt drawing-room at once became known as the Bach Choir.

Nine years later, on March 23, 1885, the Bach

Choir sang the Mass again in celebration of Bach's 200th birthday. Now, the "handful" had become a crowd. Orchestra and chorus together numbered more than 600 musicians.

Otto Goldschmidt was still the conductor, but Jenny was not a member of the chorus. She was 65 years old and content to sit in the audience and listen.

She had given her last "command performance" for Queen Victoria at Windsor in 1880. After it she had begged the Queen not to ask her to sing again.

"Let me hide my wrinkled face and gray hairs from now on," she said.

In 1881 Jenny had returned to Sweden, but not to sing. She went to receive the highest honor King Oskar II had to give: The Kingdom's Medal of Letters and Arts.

The King himself fastened the gold medal set with diamonds around Jenny's neck, saying: "Fru Jenny Lind-Goldschmidt, you have highly honored our Kingdom and our people with your matchless song. You have for long dedicated your great talent to the benefit of humanity. For these accomplishments, and in everlasting gratitude, we present you with this medal."

And then the King leaned down and kissed Jenny's cheek.

Royalty did not command Jenny to sing after 1880, but it did make a demand on her. In 1883 the Prince of Wales asked her to be the first professor of singing at the Royal College of Music.

Jenny's life was serene and happy when this photograph was taken in 1880.

Jenny taught for three years and loved every moment. But in 1866 she and Otto decided to move to the country. They bought a home in the Malvern Hills, 125 miles from London.

Once again Jenny could walk through woods and fields and hear the wild birds sing. If she wished she could try to echo the blackbird's call. Only those who loved her were around to hear her voice.

Jenny died there at Malvern on All Soul's Day, November 2, 1887. As her daughter Jenny wrote of that day later: "The sunshine came into Mother's room that last morning. I heard her greet it with some bars of a favorite song: Schumann's *Sonnenschein*."

Jenny was buried at Malvern. Her funeral was attended by many representatives of royalty as well as by many friends.

Some years later she became the first woman to have a memorial in Westminster Abbey. This was placed in the Poet's Corner beneath that of Handel, whose music she sang so movingly. The memorial bears her profile and these words from Handel's *Messiah:* "I know that My Redeemer liveth."

All the days of Jenny's life had been directed by that knowledge.

Index

Elisabeth P. Myers began to write children's stories to amuse her young son and subsequently had them published in a number of juvenile magazines. Her first book for children was published in 1961, and since that date she has written a book a year, all of which have been biographies. Mrs. Myers is a graduate of Vassar College. *Jenny Lind* is her first book for Garrard. She is presently working on another manuscript.

Mrs. Myers and her husband live in the Chicago area, where Mr. Myers is Professor of Accounting and Chairman of the Accounting Department at Northwestern University. Mrs. Myers tries to visit the locales in which her books are set. She has traveled through 48 of the 50 United States, South America, and Europe.

Frank Vaughn is a native of New Rochelle, New York. After graduating from New Rochelle schools, he attended Phoenix Art Institute in New York City. His professional career was interrupted by three years' duty in the Navy during World War II, after which he returned to New York.

Mr. Vaughn now maintains a studio in Suffern, New York where he illustrates in the commercial field and for magazines and books. He is also associated with the New York-Phoenix School of Design as an instructor of illustration and composition.

Illustrating the biography of Jenny Lind was Mr. Vaughn's first assignment from Garrard. He has given his subject a delicate, sensitive treatment, so the Swedish Nightingale emerges as a warm, living personality.

62761